Airplanes
by
Gail Saunders-Smith

Pebble Books
an imprint of Capstone Press

Pebble Books are published by Capstone Press
818 North Willow Street, Mankato, Minnesota 56001
http://www.capstone-press.com
Copyright © 1998 by Capstone Press
All Rights Reserved • Printed in the United States of America

Library of Congress Cataloging-in-Publication Data
Saunders-Smith, Gail.
  Airplanes/by Gail Saunders-Smith.
  p. cm.
  Includes bibliographical references and index.
  Summary: In simple text and photographs, describes
several different kinds of airplanes, including paper airplanes,
biplanes, and jets.
  ISBN 1-56065-498-8
  1. Airplanes--Juvenile literature. [1. Airplanes.] I. Title.

TL547.S332 1997
629.13--DC21
                                        97-23584
                                           CIP
                                           AC

Editorial Credits
Lois Wallentine, editor; Timothy Halldin and James Franklin,
design; Michelle L. Norstad, photo research

Photo Credits
Michael Green, 20
Mike Stokka, 4
Unicorn Stock/Dennis Thompson, cover, 1, 6, 8; Rod Furgason, 10
Valan Photos/Francis Lepine, 12; J.A. Wilkinson, 14, 18; Joyce
  Photographics, 16

Table of Contents

4

A paper plane
floats through the air.

A propeller plane
flies through the air.

A biplane flies
through the air.

A crop duster
flies through the air.

A seaplane flies through the air.

A water bomber
flies through the air.

16

An airline jet speeds
through the air.

A fighter jet speeds through the air.

A bomber speeds
through the air.

Words to Know

biplane—an airplane with two sets of wings

bomber—a jet that makes almost no sound and cannot be seen on radar

crop duster—an airplane used to spread chemicals over fields

fighter plane—a jet used by the military

jet—an airplane with powerful engines

paper plane—a toy airplane made of folded paper

propeller plane—an airplane with a rotating blade that moves the airplane through the air

seaplane—an airplane that takes off from and lands on water

water bomber—an airplane that dumps water on fires to help put them out

Read More

Jennings, Terry. *How Things Work: Planes, Gliders, Helicopters and Other Flying Machines.* New York: Kingfisher Books, 1993.

Johnstone, Michael. *Look Inside Cross-Sections: Airplanes.* New York: Dorling Kindersley, 1994.

Rockwell, Anne. *Planes.* New York: Dutton Children's Books, 1984.

Stephen, R. J. *The Picture World of Airliners.* New York: Franklin Watts, 1989.

Internet Sites

Kenblackburn's Home Page
http://www.geocities.com/CapeCanaveral/1817

Paper Airplane Hangar Page
http://www.tycs.demon.co.uk/planes

Seth Garner's Aviation Page
http://www.public.asu.edu/~tawny/aviation.html

USAF Aircraft
http://www.airforce.com

Note to Parents and Teachers

This book describes and illustrates various types of planes and how they move through the air. The noun changes on each page; the nouns are illustrated in the photographs. The verb describes the speed at which each plane moves. Children may need assistance in using the Table of Contents, Words to Know, Read More, Internet Sites, and Index/Word List sections of the book.

Index/Word List

Word Count: 60